CL◀SH

THE SMALLEST OF BONES

BONES

HOLLY LYN WALRATH

PRAISE FOR THE SMALLEST OF BONES

Between stars and shards of bone, Holly Lyn Walrath invites the reader to build a skeleton with her words, to get lost between the dark spaces of curved ribs. The Smallest of Bones offers so much within each poem — here, we wander beneath the moon and speak with ghosts; we transform under the night sky and haunt our own minds as the words encourage us to strip back the skin and expose rawness and vulnerability. A beautiful collection!

— SARA TANTLINGER, BRAM STOKER
AWARD-WINNING AUTHOR OF *THE
DEVIL'S DREAMLAND*

A striking meditation on the body and its ghosts, this collection is a blossoming of bones and the trauma we hold inside, a gorgeous homage to the fever dreams and nightmares we collect, break, and survive with each and every day.

— STEPHANIE M. WYTOVICH, AUTHOR
OF *THE APOCALYPTIC MANNEQUIN*

In "the smallest of bones", blood, bones, skin, and flesh are placed on the sacrificial altar as an offering to the gods, beautifully laid out to represent life's journey: love, identity, volition, pain, destruction, and finally, enlightenment.

Raw, visceral, and powerful, each word in Walrath's poems is selected with the care of a surgeon for the perfect incision. It is a journey we all walk and this is its handbook.

— CHRISTINA SNG, BRAM STOKER
AWARD WINNING AUTHOR OF
A Collection of Nightmares

For Gregory, my bone dealer

CONTENTS

THE SMALLEST OF BONES

CRANIUM

THE CRANIUM, or skull, supports the bony structures of the face, creating a cavity for the brain and shielding it from injury. The bones of the skull are linked together by sutures, small joints formed by bony ossification. At birth, the skull is made of 44 separate bones which fuse together as the body develops. Anthropologists used to argue that the brain of the female sex was similar to that of an animal. Women were emotional. Less rational than men. Women's brains were analogous to infants. Inferior. The male of the species has skulls that are, by contrast, heavier. The bone is thicker. By analyzing the key features of the skull of a dead person, a conclusion can be drawn regarding sex, but not gender. The skull and its bones may form our facial expressions, but they cannot form who we are.

if you strip me down to my bones
am I yours?

there are few places left
that man has not touched

we square cities, parks
but long for wildness

let us not assign
too much power
to the virgins

buildings have ghosts
but so do trees

where the demon's tongue
is rough like a cat's
how I strain against it

I told the demon I loved you
she stood over the water
and whispered a word—
brought down the mountain

what is a demon anyway
but a flushed girl
with ocean eyes

poured heat over my skin
like bleach
      there were graces I wanted to say over
      your body
           but there was nothing left for me
           to pray

you say

the smallest of bones
is a part of the hammer in your ear

love is a heartbreak you can hear

god doesn't interest me
only other worlds than this

if I am trapped in hell
                    I will miss you most

we are the tree burning
afterwards, there is nothing
left of us but black ash

sea fog haunts me
like memory
stealing over the bay

what is the price of water?

I sink myself in the river at dawn
your words are the stones
in my pockets

sunlight is a eulogy
for the way we once were
all tangled up together at night

I was the moon peeking
through your window
watching you sleep
memorizing your stripped body

I wanted to eat your dreams

when I die, you say
donate my body to science
so kids can pull on my nerves

take my ashes up like paste
warmed by your skin
rub me across your hands

the clouds are wild in the sky
I want to hold you between my teeth
what would you say to some foreplay
loud and vibrating like the cicadas
slick around your golden boy hips

at the top of the mountain
we collapse, lungs grasping,
into the graves of moths

ask me, where is your wild woman?

I shot her in the face

She's wandering the valley
of my ribs
skull turned inside out

we made love in the snow
layers of puffy material between us
looking up at the dark mirror of the sky

the thing I miss most about our world is the stars

MANDIBLE

THE MANDIBLE OR jawbone is the largest and strongest bone in the face of the human species. It binds the lower teeth in place. The word derives from the Latin word mandibula, plainly "used for chewing." The body of the mandible is curved and from the inside, the mandible seems concave. Like a womb. At birth, the body of the bone is a mere shell, but in old age, the bone can become greatly reduced in volume due to loss of teeth from violence or decay. When human remains are found, the mandible is sometimes the only recognizable bone. Fractures of this bone are the most common in cases of domestic violence. The fist is a favorite tool for assaults. The mandibles of the female of the species are smaller. Thinner. Rounder. More obtuse. Straight. Straight. Straight.

you're always in your head
thinking happy thoughts
light-struck, body contorted
in the clouds

when I go out at night
I dig in the St. Augustine
until I can think straight
or sink my fingers in ants

your mouth tastes like chaos
bourbon-sweet

harder than obsidian

no one else will remember
the soft way you sleep
when you are gone

so I will tell your ghost

who stands on my side of the bed
and kisses my hair as I sleep

how I snuck into the black hole
between your jaw and sinus

how I wanted to hear you sing

broken into a thousand shards
I wander in your fields
hands soaked with the blood
of your light

moon, come closer
let me crawl up into your mouth
hold me under your tongue

like unspoken regret

you sleep beside me
warm and constant
like the holy moon

and I laid there in the stars
I drew every one up to my belly
pressed them into my skin

one
        by star-struck
                one

the skeleton birds came in the morning
waking, they all out to me
land on my arms like feeble longing
groom my hair, whisper in my ear

the bodies of the skeleton birds
are porous
like the minds of womenfolk

you asked me to stop
singing to them at night
I left you in the morning

under threat, I cast off my breasts
vestigial organs
regenerated autonomically
with little or no scarring

when one member of a social group
considers itself a burden it may commit
self-destruction

some parasites
infect their hosts
until they have control
of their minds
at which point

they drown themselves

honestly, I'd like to know what it's like
to love a woman as a woman
I'd like to be honest

honestly, I'd like to know what it's like
to be a woman

see how you're still fucking me up
even now that you're a ghost

these secrets you carry for me,
are they too heavy?

to love so much your body changes
curving together like two halves of the taijitu
or the earth and the moon
must be dreadful and excruciating

STERNUM

THE STERNUM IS A LONG, flat bone in the chest. It connects the ribs via cartilage and forms the front of the rib cage, thus protecting the heart, lungs, and major blood vessels from injury. It is shaped like a necktie. Fractures of the sternum are rather rare. They may result from trauma, such as the impact of a steering wheel in a car accident. Some studies reveal that repeated punches or continual beatings, sometimes called "breastbone punches" to the sternum area can cause fracture. Dislocation of this bone is rare and usually caused by severe trauma. The sternum is also called the breast bone. Hiding our hearts is easy when we have so many bones.

you shouldn't love so much
you know ghosts don't have feelings

I wish I could hurt you
the way you hurt me
but my skin is a mask
and my fists are flowers

I reach out
but never get a hold on you

you say something about Nietzsche

there's only this

for now,   remember me
        by this

take it into your hands warm it
with your breath

        hold it close
        before it dies

condemned women
are rare birds
we should study them

      I carry my face in my pocket

            when I need to, I can become
            the type of woman you want
            this is not a skin, but myself

digging us out of the sand
he said, this body is camouflage

his hands tensile
slipping under my radar
my heart was sonar

I let pieces of myself
orbit this moon

they beg for their bodies back
these women who are poor
and we look down on them
we say, you don't really need that
do you?

the most beautiful part of being
          broke
was curling up beside you in the fever
          sick
with the fear of losing one of us

          I didn't really
                    care
          which one of us
                    died
          first so long as
                    we did

a man
once asked me how I got so thin
I told him I was made of glass

when you're metal
your either hard or flexible
those are the two choices
there's nothing in-between

you pounded out my body
until it was pliable
and then you made it something
beautiful

is your heart breaking
to see me?

SACRUM

FORMED by the fusing of sacral vertebrae, the sacrum is a large, triangular bone at the base of the spine. It is situated between the two hard wings of the pelvis. Curved upon itself, the base of the sacrum careens forward. Before the adoption of the word sacrum, the bone was called *holy* in Greek, "hieron osteon" and was used for animal sacrifice. In females of the species, the sacrum is shorter and wider. Researchers comment on how this is more valuable to childbearing. Because even our bones are made for what men want. Because as hard as we try to be sacred, they can always use us for sacrifice. In Greek, "hieron" also meant "temple." Within its bony concavity hides the ovaries and uterus, the sacred organs of procreation. Thanks to its great size, the sacrum is usually the last bone of a buried body to rot.

you meander through my dreams
like the ghost you made out of my future

we are bottled up
with each other
and the message

there's a town born underwater
and all the people know how to really breathe
but I don't speak this current language

I used to listen to your music on repeat
until I discovered all the cuts it was leaving
in the hidden places, my thighs and calves,
so I stopped putting myself in that position
but pain is like a melody you can't forget

there was this girl I knew who believed in love
and she took up arms, she took up arms,
but when it came time to fight all she found
in her arms was a bouquet of pain

when you leave me

in the landfills
hotel rooms
temples
and canyons
I feel—

      peaceful for a moment
my mind rests on some
slim idea of beauty
and then discomfort
slips in like a needle
like—

      the riot of my body
         displayed
            in all its
                un-glory

you hold a light up to your teeth
see how transparent I've become
I put my breast in your mouth
to shut you up

I grew you in a tank
cartilage and soft spines
othering you gives me pleasure
that and the taste of your smile

aren't we still primitive
you asked me in bed
aren't we still ancestors

and say
my name again
say it into my skin

carve it on my bones
even the ones I don't use
like my hips

am I holy
if I am not a temple
am I human

we must love
like
a story like
poetry

we must love

SPINE

THE HUMAN VERTEBRAL COLUMN, also known as the backbone or spine, is built from thirty-three vertebrae. The spine curves and curves and curves. The lumbar curve is more marked in the female of the species. The arresting segmented pattern of the spine is established when the embryo begins to form. Functionally, the vertebral column encases and protects the spinal cord, part of the central nervous system. If the vertebral bones are shattered, the spinal cord can be punctured by sharp fragments of bone. A victim might only suffer loss of hand or foot function. Call me victim again. Evolutionary psychology suggests that heterosexual men might be on the lookout for a very specific kind of spine in sexual partners. Are they looking for weakness or strength. Maybe we should stop looking for men as partners.

you are strong and wild
like the mountain and the sky
I believe in you

I believe in you

you are strong and wild

I am grasping at bits of bone
holding them up to my mouth
grief is a memory

first I cut away my face
and then I held the flowers
up to the empty space

have you ever crushed
a peony in your hand
have you ever loved
something so much
you needed to destroy it

a woman with no skin
peers at me
out of the mirror

how do I know I am a woman?

my love is vestigial now
the final segment of a spine
broken and scattered
across the marshes

CALCANEUS

THE CALCANEUS or heel bone is part of the tarsus of the foot which constitutes the heel. It is the largest bone of the foot. The muscles which insert on the calcaneus aid in walking, running, and jumping. In Greek mythology, the hero Achilles was dipped into the River Styx by his mother, Thetis. She held his heel and slowly lowered her wriggling little boy into the magical torrent. The place she touched became his weakness. In China, women's feet were broken and folded at the arch, bound tight and sewn with bandages. The perfect feet were considered *jinlian* or "lotus" feet. What we call beauty and pain are not so different. Young bones are soft. If you land on your feet from a fall, your body's weight can drive the talus bone into the calcaneus. As a rule, the greater the impact, the more the calcaneus is damaged.

my body is two-thirds
whiskey
and one-third
ghosts

cyanide
is the fuel
of lost dreamers

after you said this
I knew I chose wrong
but I still loved the fuck out of you

maybe I'm the problem

and I'm fine with this
stripping my skin to the wind
so we can walk in the night

I just wish I knew which way
to go when I get lost

I just wish you were okay with men

help me blow on this dandelion
I said, as we knelt naked in the field
we have to wish for something
don't we?

look, pain is this human thing
and without it we would be skeletons
but that doesn't mean we have to die
without saying I love you

you put your heel over my lips
toes sinking into my eyes
and your bones smelled
dry and dusty

I've always been a woman without hands

you put me on the windowsill
and then you said things like, jump little bitch.
So I guess what I'm saying is, I know how to jump
for men

on the rocks the ocean froths
dashing itself against the earth
haunted like myself

and sometimes I pray for you I can't help it
it's something they taught me

      I learned how to hate my body
      and the things I want
      gotta hate those most of all

           I still laugh when I remember
           the sacrifice you made
           just to be able to make love
           to me without carrying
           that sack of guilt

the smallness of you
slack in my hand
I wrap bone chains
around your head

I cut off my hair
and light it
with your silver
zippo

the very preciousness of you
beside me and sleeping

god I love the things I hate

TEMPORAL

THE TEMPORAL BONES are located at the sides and base of the skull and house the structures of the ears. Exact etymology is unknown, but the word is thought to be from the French *temporal* meaning "earthly" which is directly from the Latin *tempus* meaning "time, proper time, or season." There is also a connection with the Greek word *temnion*, to wound in battle. Fractures of the temporal bone are associated with head injuries. Bleeding from the ear. The female sex of the species has a smaller bony labyrinth, a cavity on the temporal bone that protects the tissue for hearing and balance. Men use only one side of their brains to listen. That doesn't mean one sex is better or more capable than the other, no matter what they tell you. If you keep listening to what they tell you you are, soon enough you become that thing.

there's everything and then there's poetry
Poem, you caught me up in your hands
and said if you keep moaning like that
I'm going to lose it

I think we write about ourselves so we can
become creatures

we wish we could get out of our skin
wouldn't you rather be something violent
if you had the choice

fuck what other people say
If I need to sell my soul
at least it's mine to give

or maybe we're just broken
like bloody pixie sticks
and we just need someone
to pick us up and eat us

if loving you means I must die

I love you
I love you
I love you

a thousand times I love you

come back to haunt me
I don't want to think about
what I mean without you,
what kind of woman that
makes me

if you slowly bend a bone
over time, inch by inch
it deforms until it molds
to your hands

it will all make sense in the end
the love and the pain

after death, I mean

ACKNOWLEDGMENTS

"Sacrum" first appeared in Barely South Review. The section poems for this book were inspired by old anatomy books, and, occasionally, Wikipedia entries that had out of date information about the human body. I adapted phrases from these into found poems for the spine of these poems.

I am supremely grateful to the CLASH Books team and Leza Cantoral for taking a chance on this weird little book. Thanks to Joel Amat Güell for creating a cover to go along with this little beast.

Much love is owed to the people who support my writing and weird shenanigans: James Walrath, who will always be there to make a good bone joke with me. Thanks to my critique group members Cassandra Rose Clarke, Michael Glazner, Chun Lee, and Kevin

O'Neill. Other folks who are a huge part of my writing community include the kind folks at SFPA, Writespace, Codex, Interstellar Flight Press, and the HWA dark poets, Rachel Walrath, Presley Thomas, Jamie Danielle Portwood, Jeremy Brett, Tony Clavelli, Kyle Russell, Chloe Clark, Leslie McCoy Archibald, Jef Rouner, Amy Archambault, Lisa Kiernan, Deborah Davitt, Michelle Muenzler, Kate Pentecost, Patty Flaherty Pagan, Lee Steiner, John Bernhard, Lois Stark, and many more. There are too many of you lovely souls to count.

And especial thanks to Jody Townsley Morse for bringing me bones and treasures for inspiration.

ABOUT THE AUTHOR

Holly Lyn Walrath's poetry and short fiction appears in *Strange Horizons*, *Fireside Fiction*, *Daily Science Fiction*, Liminality, and *Analog*. She is the author of *Glimmerglass Girl* (Finishing Line Press, 2018), winner of the Elgin Award for best speculative chapbook, and *Numinose Lapidi*, a chapbook in Italian from Kipple Press. She holds a B.A. in English from The University of Texas and a Master's in Creative Writing from the University of Denver. You can find her canoeing the bayou in Houston, Texas, on Twitter @HollyLynWalrath, or at www.hlwalrath.com.

WE PUT THE LIT IN LITERARY

CLASHBOOKS.COM

TWITTER

IG

FB

@clashbooks

Email

clashmediabooks@gmail.com

Publicity

McKenna Rose

clashbookspublicity@gmail.com

NAKED

Joel Amat Güell